a peace... for you

Warren...

The world needs more people that are willing to stop... and share a moment of their time - Thanks so much.

God Bless! 9/30/17

Stephen Davis

a peace... for you

Kitra Martindavis

a peace... for you

Cover art: *Twisted* by Kyler O. Davis
Cover design: Michael K. French
Photo Credit: Tasha Fuller

Editor: T. Carol Patterson
Special Mention: Dr. Ritchie Carroll
Special Mention: Kathy (Durben) Welsch

ISBN: 154532753x
ISBN 13: 978-1545327531

Publishing: Artik Expressions

www.Artikexpressions.com

Dedication…

This one,

this one right here…

                had to be for me

but…

it's also for my three!

*Welcome to **a peace... for you.***

As you delve into these pages you will notice my personal style as an artist to visually create a flow of energy, thought and emotion. The lulls and breaks, the emphasized or de-emphasized words and phrases are all intentional. The unconventional phrasing and spacing might suggest you pause, but pausing is not required.

Occasionally, I find myself having an additional or second thought within a sentence, so I include it as if it is exactly that, a second thought.

Introduction

My journey of writing has at times been surreal, but I have come to accept them as not being random, but for a reason. I am often inspired to write a poem, a simple thought or a short story. When inspired to write a *peace* spelled **P-E-A-C-E**, I have accepted that it is meant to either invoke a peace-filled mindfulness for myself or someone else. It may be for someone I have yet to cross paths with; so, I can't and don't claim or feel that I own all the *peace's* that I have written and those that are still to come.

I have learned, and now understand that everything I write is intended for someone, but not everything I write is intended for everyone. At least not intended for their pleasure but sometimes... it is intended for their pain (NOT TO CAUSE PAIN) but intended for them to recognize their pain and then, the invocation of *peace*.

So here I am, giving you a *peace* that God gave to me, for me..., but also, for me to give to you.

Love & Acknowledgement

First giving honor to God... thank you for considering me.

To my husband, it has been a journey and I am ever so grateful that you love me despite me. Although you may not have always understood the meaning behind the *peaces*, you have always supported my writing effort and helped me realize the need to share them with others. I... love you.

To my boys "hey man," l-i-v-e your lives like you mean to and like you need to. "**You will find it...you will recognize it... because HE is going to show it to you.**" Promise to always look after, take care of and love each other – no matter what, because that is what family does. I love you but know that God loves you more.

Love and respect to mommy and daddy. I cannot begin to express how grateful I am that you both are simply who you are. If either of you were any different then I might be too. To all my siblings and the rest of my family, thank you for your love and support. You have always accused me of being long winded, and you were right.

To all my friends…, even as I begin this section of acknowledgements tears literally fill my eyes. Having crossed paths with each one of you, has forever changed me. Truly, the sun shines differently! I am afraid that if I were to attempt to acknowledge everyone personally, I would omit someone.

I need you all to know that you have been a tremendous encouragement through my life's journey. Please understand that as we shared with one another over the years, and then I put "pen to paper" that it was intended and written for *peace*.

My love… to you all.

Peaces

a peace... to love and to live
pages 1-68

a peace... to heal and to forgive
pages 71-119

a peace...
to love and to live

In My Path

I was walking along a path one day

        …and there you were

          not in my   way

just

in

my

path…

and

I

thank

God!

My Wish for You

today
I wish for you enough love
so you will desire to love someone back

today
I wish for you enough heartache
so you will know that love is real

today
I wish for you enough confidence
so you know that you are competent

today
I wish for you enough patience
so you understand that life... doesn't revolve
around you

today
I wish for you enough curiosity
so you will not become stagnant

today
I am wishing you enough determination
in all that you do
so you will persevere in your life's desires

today
I wish for you enough independence
so you will never become dependent
on anyone or anything

today
I wish you enough sensitivity
so you know how to be compassionate
and humble, and know that love is real

today
I wish for you enough satisfaction
so you will not envy or covet that of your
brother's and sister's

my greatest wish for you today is enough faith

so
your
future
is
secure

Choose To

When God allows your eyes to open
with or without sight   *choose to*

when God allows your legs to move
with or without assistance   *choose to*

when God allows you to sip a cup of coffee
a glass of juice or plug in your oxygen tank
choose to

when heading out for the day
whether going to work or going to play
choose to

Choose   to create positive energy within
yourself
even when you're feeling tapped out

Choose   to see the glass half full instead of
half empty

Choose   to love others without forgetting to
love yourself

Choose to

Choose   to give HIM the glory… and
recognize your blessings

because it is…   a Choice

Legacy

1st, 2nd and 3rd generation…
blood running deep & warm

is thicker than
hamburger and tomato gravy
before you add the…   "hush your mouth chile"

Strong men &
women bearing strong men &
women all coming from   ***mama&papa***

who if you ask, were saints if anyone knew one

I have only met **them** *(*RIPP)* … in my dreams

but see them daily when I see and talk to the

strong men &
women that are the

1st

2nd

and 3rd generation…   of a legacy of love

****Rest in Perfect Peace***

5

Ma'dear

I understand what you meant
when you said I would never understand
but I do comprehend

I know how you felt
when you felt like you would melt
into a puddle of mud

You know...   you and me

we both see something
that we know we see

just   can't   put our finger on it

or then again...   have we?

"Call it what you want...

  itiswhatitis

  unmistakeningly

  itiswhatitis

                          ... *life*"

Just Being Me

Since childhood, everyone always told me I
was different

mommy would say "born years late" and "girl,
you look at life through rose colored glasses"

It has been those two things that have made
me the woman I am

and although I don't think that I am wise…

others think so

But the consummate optimist, that, I know I am

"Mind over matter, I say… and
it is what it is   and
sometimes, it just ain't what it ain't"

love life

love others

love yourself

Connectivity

The draw, the connection, it was immediate
from the start

It's like…   you had always been a part
not of just any past but specifically of mine
like a friendship that had already stood
the test of time

Like a familiar pair of jeans, or a familiar scent

you say   "it's like I was assigned to you"
I say   "unexplainable, it was just meant"

The connection, the draw, it was immediate
from the get

just couldn't put my finger on…
but now I think I get it

Phenomenal energy
simply   connectedusfromtheget

you say   "it's like I was assigned to you"
I say   "like metal to magnet"

                connectedfromtheget

Trust

I've
been
walking wondering
seeking searching
longing lodging

I've
been
pondering perpetrating paining
dodging drinking drowning
breaking burning barfing

I
want to
live laugh love
sing smile survive

I've
gotta
tug
trust and

try

Artik I

blessed & purposed
purposed & blessed

recognize & accept it

Artik II

life…

is about relevancy

who and what is relevant in your life…?

Dare

i dare you to seek to love others
and
i dare you to believe that people
are "good" by nature

i dare you to trust that you can do
what you need to do when you
need to do it
and
i dare you to receive your purpose
in life

… i double dare you

Aware

Don't lose yourself
in someone else's
life

and

Don't lose yourself
because of someone else's
love

You Know Me... Do You Love Me

I am you   and you…   you are me

We are His children   and

We are His greatest Creation

made   in His Likeness

made   in His Image

made   according to His Will

Psalms 139:14: *"I will praise You, for I am fearfully and wonderfully made; Marvelous are Your works, And that my soul knows very well."*

You know me   and I…   I know you

neither of us

are worthy   of His Grace or Mercy and we

haveallsinnedandfallenshortoftheGloryofGod

Mark 12:31: *"The second is this, Love your neighbor as yourself. There is no commandment greater than these."*

So...

am I	and are you loving
do I	and do you have joy
are we	peaceful... and patient
do we	show kindness... and goodness
are we	faithful
do we	show gentleness and self control
and do	we walk in the Spirit

do I...?

do you...?

**I am your neighbor   and
the lesbian, gay, bi-sexual and transgender
is your neighbor**

You...are my neighbor...

I love you, but... do you love me?

Just Perfect

What if…

God made each one of us imperfect
just so that we would learn to
accept and love each other

just

as

we

are

He does

In Motion

I don't know how to sit still
for long periods of time

I am afraid… that I might have

an unsettled   spirit

Sometimes… that scares me!

I am unsure what it means

to always need or want

to
be

in

motion

Understanding Love

I was thinking that

I was   *confused*   but

I am learning that the more I live

the more I learn about   love
love   can be complicated

despite drugsalcohol and ignorance
despite someone beingmeanbeingstubborn
beingrudebeingplainhateful

I have always heard that there is someone for
everyone

and I guess that's true

…whether they are the perfect someone is
another story

but…

I am learning the more I live

the more I learn

that I too   am not perfect

Be All Right

be all right

as the sun rises
promising opportunities of a brand-new day

be all right
as the day progresses
with challenges that are not insurmountable

everything will be   all right

as i soar and shine
like the ray of sunshine i am

... and I will always be   all right

Powerful and Able

We… are empowered

thus

capable to do
and
responsible to say

charged
to
walkhandinhandwitheachother

in order to speak
into each other's lives
and
be instrumental in
helping others

to
walk in wisdom
as we trust
and
as we believe

to
walk in wisdom
as we grow
and
as we achieve

to
walk in wisdom
as we live our lives

as

Women

in

Christ!

Sistah

I learned from the woman that you were
but have grown & am empowered by the
woman you have become

As the younger sister
I always wanted to be just like you
and as a grown woman
I now know that I am the woman I am
because of you

I could always see...
a quiet strength within you
but the strength you now scream
is intoxicating, exhilarating and most of all...
liberating

Artik III

the reality of it is
　…is the reality of it

*some people hated to hear me say "it is what it
is," so this is my new mantra*

Artik IV

i… am peace-filled

and *it* "fills"… so good

Loving You

I forgive you for the father that you were
and   for the father that you weren't

I am ever so grateful

and

I love you

for the father

that
you

are

Ordained

I…   have been ordained

not ordained to preach
or prophesy   *(or even to be a Deaconess)*
but ordained nonetheless…   by God Himself

I…   have an insatiable desire

not desire but   need
given to me nonetheless   by God Himself

I used to try not to
but just can't help myself

I just have to speak

I just have to share

I just have to see…   and help others see
see something in themselves
see something in others

some   thing   anything
anyonethingortwo

that can help
                     connect
                     protect
                     correct
                     eject

26

but never   neglect

anyonethingortwo
in themselves or in others

God needs...   no   He desires
God desires us to have an insatiable need
to accept our
in
  di...   vidual

calling

our
in
  di...   vidual

speaking of the tongue experiences
(no - i didn't say experiments)

embrace them for what they are
embrace them
for what they   are supposed to be
...our own
in
  di...   vidual

our own
per-son-al
per = through
Son = Jesus
al   = having the character of

ordination

Some Other Time

no, I wasn't sleeping
just in deep thought
sometimes
I can get
lost doing this

…thinking
about this
or   that
sometimes regressing to where I've been
or   pretending to be somewhere I'm not
or even
someone else…

someone stronger
than i
tougher
than **ME**

someone like
let's see

a Black Superwoman

yeah
you too…?

I thought I

was the only   one

The Perfect Dream

I cried myself awake this morning

after

dreaming

of

world peace & love

Hugs and Kisses

I love...

    how you

      ling

            er

on my lips...

when I leave   you

never a good bye
just a see you soon

I get lost...

    in your embrace

reminiscing about my childhood
and how you stood...

10ft tall

when all   seemingly rested on your

shoulders

I feel safe...

safest
     in your presence

capable of

competent to do

charged to be

confident

tough...

but

tender

trained to give

good

hugs and kisses

Me

i… am a highly positive person
i… am peaceful
i… am loving
i… am kind
i… am generous

i… do speak to others without knowing who
they are
i… do check on my neighbors, when i haven't
seen them for a while and when they cross my
mind or heart
i… do sometimes pay for the items of the
person in front of or behind me in line
i… do give compliments when it's obvious and
even when it's not
i… do call my friends and relatives to keep up
with them even when my number has also "not
changed"

*i… love to be around others, but recognize
when i need to be alone*

i… want to be infectious not "toxic"
i… want to promote peace&love not hate&war
i… want to see others do well and thrive
i… want&choose to live a positive life   and
i… want all of the above for you   too

Strength, Power & Admiration

I am not a basketball fan but...

I was blessed one day to watch ESPN's "E:60."
The title of the program was "Penny Saved"
and it was about Penny Hardaway and his
good friend Desmond Merriweather.

As they interviewed Desmond during the
difficult time of him dealing with Stage IV Colon
Cancer, he had to take a break from the
camera and when he returned, the interviewer
asked, "Are you not feeling well?"
"Um huh" he said.
"Did you just get sick," she asked.
"Yes" he said quickly.   *(the Strength)*
"Why do you do this," she asked?
"It's for the kids," he said.   *(the Power)*
"I mean, it's taking so much out of you,"
she said.
"But...
it puts so much in me," he replied. *(the Admiration)*

*(*RIPP Mr. Merriweather)*

33

Reunion/New Union

unfamiliar

        faces

unknown

        places

blood running warm

love deep rooted

unityeverlasting!

Artik V

love others…

(period)

35

Artik VI

accept things for what they are
then
except things for what they are not

receive things to be the positive force they are

then

*exclude the things that you have recognized
are not – a positive force*

Let Me Introduce Myself
(re-visioning "Some Other Time")

No,

I wasn't sleeping... just in deep thought
Sometimes, I can get lost doing this

thinking and pondering

about this or that...
sometimes regressing to where I've been
other times
just thinking about where I'd rather be

most times...

I am simply preparing to propel...
to catapult myself

in a whole new direction
with   a purposed intention

there is no one   tougher than I
no one...   stronger

I..   I am   Superwoman

you too...

I ain't surprised

Naiveté

I thought   he was her pimp
or   her drug dealer
I would have never imagined in a trillion years
that   he was her boyfriend

He was much older than she
                          old enough to be her dad
maybe even her granddad

I could not comprehend it as a child
that   he could love her like we did
                      he… had a choice
                      he wasn't family and
                      he… didn't have

bloodrunningdeep…
throughhisveinstoconnectthem

                          he… had a choice

But I guess so did we
and some   opted out

I guess   they… didn't know how to deal
didn't know   how to love beyond
the worry and pain she caused

you could cut it with a knife
…it was so thick   the pain

38

it would grab
grandmamommyandauntie's hearts
and probably most of all... uncle's **soul**
(he couldn't protect her like the warrior he was supposed to be)

you could cut it with a knife
...it was so thick   the pain...

causing instantaneous wrinkles in their
foreheads

causing instantaneous hunching in their backs
twitching in their muscles like they were the
ones shooting up in their veins

legs... dragging the pain like they were the
ones that had been stabbed at the base of their
back

their hearts... s k i p p i n g b e a t s like they
were on uppers

and...

their stomachs fluttering with waves of nausea
on the   verge
on   the   verge

ontheverge of   throwing up
the lil' bits of food that they were able to take in
(haven't had a full meal in Lord knows when)

I could not for the life of me…
comprehended it as a child

that   he could love her like we did
                      he wasn't family and
                      he… didn't have

bloodrunningdeep…
throughhisveinstoconnectthem

but he…
knew how to deal…
knew how to love her beyond the pain
she caused
…it was so thick   the pain

but now…

I

understand

Get Thee Behind Me

Just when I thought I was safe

and I thought…
I knew it without a shadow of doubt

Satan came and tried me

(so glad I know from whence cometh my help ~ Psalm 121:2-3)

41

Enjoying

I enjoy
a bad glass of wine

Can you really tell the difference   I can't

I enjoy
a nice   quiet   spot curledupwithabook

I enjoy
sitting in the midst of others choosing solitude
when it's convenient

and
            sometimes   even when
it's rude

I enjoystrugglingtowrite…

            sometimes   having no clue

what it all means

and other times

not wanting to admit

the realities of what I have just

re

        gur

   gi   tated

on paper

but still
enjoy…

I enjoy Life

He Is

Do you see him
… do you see the man before you

Now of course, that was a rhetorical question
but again, I ask… do you see him

He…

is a man
of
faith
and
integrity

a man of
compassion…
and
of
courage

a man
of
affection and ambition

a diplomatic man

a generous and gentle
hard-working
intelligent man

a kind
loving
loyal man

a passionate
patient
reliable
warm-hearted

and tough   man

he... is all that

so we should recognize and acknowledge

...when we see him

God's Will

truth is…
if God isn't moving you to do something
then He's probably telling you to
b e   s t i l l

(be still)

And…?

What if…

I am the only one that understands you

and…

you're the only one that understands me

what then…?

Ma'dear II

Not only do I understand what you meant
when you said I would never understand

…but I can also relate

I must admit…

that I've been in a state

of confusion…
a state of illusion
a state of   delusion
to the point
that I'm almost at
a state   of   explosion
and have experienced
…a bit of erosion

So you see…

I know how you felt

when you felt like you would melt
into a puddle of mud

and truth be told

…we both could see
what it was we were trying not to see

and yeah,

we could put our fingers on it then
just didn't want to

… did we?

unbelievable

life…

or should I say

just

truly

livin'

I Miss You

I miss
hearing you call me
Kee-Chops

so…
sister calls me that
every now and then

and it makes me smile

Recognize

Embrace
Celebrate
Rejoice
for what things are

and then ...

Rejoice
Celebrate
Embrace
for what things are not

Love

Living

On   a

Virtually

Empty

          earth

Living
On   a
Virtually
Empty

          earth

Love?

Artik VII

h
   c
 a
e
r

for the vibe

people try to figure out why I am so positive …
it's because I reach for it

Artik VIII

I am not so random

and

neither

are

you

Artik IX

it may not be all that I want it to be
but I am making the best of

...what it is

Beauty Unexpected

I saw the three of them as they walked toward the front of the building, with that cutie of a spanutie little boy.

Then, I watched the father walk around with him once, twice, three times as lil' fella stopped, picked up leaves, picked up sticks, picked up what looked like a piece of a discarded cup, as it headed towards his mouth.

The father must have gotten tired of the constant stop and go, the explore and… explore some more when he picked lil' fella up and carried him back to the front of the building.

As I headed out for lunch, I came face to face with the three of them, father #1, father #2 and lil' fella. "What a cutie of a spanutie he is," I said to them. They explained that lil' fella was their 2nd adoption. And…, that he was local from Montgomery County. They told me his name and the name of their 1st child who was also a boy.

When I opened my mouth, what came out was how blessed they were, and how blessed the two little boys were to have been adopted… to have been given a chance to be loved & cared for. I shared with them that I too have two sons and felt equally blessed to have been given a chance to love and be loved.

I was so happy for them.

Lil' fella began smiling and waved at me, as he jumped into my arms. I held him briefly but felt the love... he smelled like my boys at his age.

beautiful little hand I thought   and
beautiful little teeth
beautiful lil' fella
beautiful... daddy #1
beautiful... daddy #2

As we parted, daddy #2 said, "hey, can I give you a hug?" We embraced and my heart just about exploded.

Memories of A Big O' Woman

I got up early on Saturday morning and headed to the store. List in hand, I ventured into aisles and rounded corners that featured sale items and bargains, I seemingly could not pass up.

I spent more time than I had. I had things to do, people to see, places to go. However, I started thinking about ingredients, recipes, mouth-watering homemade family specialties, and passed down traditional dishes. I started reminiscing about hours spent in her hot kitchen and have vivid memories of old cloth calendar dish towels, cast iron skillets, pot & pans, lard and of auntie's favorite "purple" tin cup. I thought about her burning her hands but pressing on, as if she never felt it.

She'd cut mold off old cheese and pinch mold off old bread; "Smell that before you throw it away girl; it's probably still good," she would say. I became a pro in the smelling department. *(maybe that's why I have issues with odors now)*

She had to have been the biggest woman I ever laid eyes on, at least 20ft. tall and she certainly weighed more than a pound. Standing and walking around as though she could carry the weight of the world on her shoulders. She even slept with authority and power, only succumbing long enough to figure out what she had to accomplish the next day which often consisted of tending to Ms. Binnie, checking in on Mrs. Smith or helping Aunt Betty bake cakes.

She would run from store to store to get the "best buy" because she always wanted the most for her money. Daddy called her "General" and I am not completely sure why. Was it her commanding nature or because it appeared as if she ran a general store? People could and would stop by when in need of groceries and she seemingly had an endless supply of everything. She had extra soda and canned goods under and behind beds. The multipurpose baking soda, soap, toilet tissue, toothpaste, Tussie deodorant, even extra clothes, to include underwear, bras, shoes... Stuff..., stuffed in the bathroom closets. Stuff..., stuffed in the foot locker in auntie's room, and more stuff in the rusted cabinet on the back porch. Stuff..., in every nook and cranny. But I came to realize... that it wasn't just stuff. It was all useful; it was all needed. Maybe not needed by any of us but needed by someone, someone important- like a hitch-hiker or one of the Gypsies that came through town. Like I said, an endless supply of everything.

It was like... she was always feeding a multitude. I am certainly not comparing her to

Jesus but, there was always enough and always some left… to share. "Run across the street and take a plate... don't forget to go up and then down, making sure to drop off extra rolls to Mr. Clive," she would say. *(Mr. Clive sure loved apple butter but his glass eye scared me.)* He sure could pick some blackberries though, as he hauled us around Z-ville every year, always finding the best berry picking spots.

Let me tell you…, by the time I finished drifting in and out of the aisles of the store and drifting in… and out… of the memories of her and her kitchen, I didn't need another thing and my cart was overflowing.

Suddenly… out of everywhere, I could see and feel her just as if she had been the one sending me to the store with her list. It was there, in the last aisle…, packages of butt ends of meats and cheeses at a discounted price... so low that anyone could afford 'em.

"Hey Grams, I feel you... I feel your presence. I… am so proud to be a part of you, counting it a blessing to have so many memories of time spent. You teaching… and me learning… me watching… and you showing me how I too, could become a Big O' Woman."

Artik X

Just because it's not your truth
doesn't make it a lie

The Tram Ride

They caught my eye as they boarded the tram.
Both slightly bent over, osteoporosis perhaps.
She more girth than he; he taller than she.
Had never seen either of them before but they
seemed to fit perfectly together with their
tattered clothes and shoes run over. Her hair
and hands looked as though they belong to a
centenarian and his, not far behind. Caught a
glimpse of her teeth as she talked slowly, just
above a whisper and I assumed that his
matched hers - few there and rotten those that
were.

*"Wait… a minute… what – what is that
smell?"*

Why am I straining to hear what she is saying?
She is not talking to me, she's clearly talking to
him. She doesn't enunciate well enough for me
to understand, but he listens attentively,
looking at her while rubbing & patting her
hands gently. He appears to be taking in
everything she's saying… maybe she's
speaking a foreign language and that's why the
words are incomprehensible to me.

I am quickly intrigued by these two, their
closeness, their oneness, her sitting almost in
his lap. He welcomes her, accepts, and clearly
responds to her in a way that is… that is

more… than attentive. It is like a love affair. They steal kisses and look into each other's eyes as if no one else is around.

"OMG, did she just put her hand on his obviously not so private area?" I tell myself, "Look away."

Just at that moment, he begins to caress her breasts. Okay, now I know that these folks are grown and they both have to be at least 80 years old plus. My mind shouts so loud that obviously, others around hear me and all agree, "Get a room!" Do people this age really still have sex? Can they still have sex? Well, it's none of my business and maybe I'm just a prude because I just don't get into PDA.

"What is that smell…? Is that his breath?"
(I hear and strangely feel him moan.)

Okay, now I am way too deep into their business. I know a hard on when I see one and it appears he has one! At his age? On this tram ride that should have been over seemingly hours ago. We're just going from one side of the airport to another so that I can get to Gate D, so I can get to the West Coast. I have never been to the…

"OMG…! No, she is not… yes, she is… she is jacking him off and looks like she knows what she's doing. Well, I guess it's like riding a bike. But here? Now? Why? How

can they be so free to do what they are doing in front of all of us?"

Something deep inside of me or at least down below prevents me from moving, prevents me from discontinuing this shared intimate experience they are having or should I say that I am having with them. I certainly would have chosen to opt out had I known!

"What... is.... that....... smell, am I the only one who smells it? I know that I am a little hypo-sensitive to odors but OMG!"

Finally, we are about to stop. This tram-ride-love-affair is just about to end. As I hear him moan again I hear her moan simultaneously. Don't tell me, they have both climaxed just in time to exit the tram... Unbelievable! The automated voice comes over the speaker saying that this tram is now out of service and everyone must exit. We all begin shuffling vying for immediate exodus. But I notice them.

"Am I the only one still intrigued by these two?"

The couple now sits motionless, or so it seems that they both sit motionless. I see him reach up and wipe a tear from his cheek and cover his mouth – seemingly in agony. He... is crying and she... she isn't paying him any attention. He seems oddly, strangely, painfully,

& pitifully alone. My intrigue has now turned to concern as I ask him if they need any assistance. He longingly looks at her then looks through me and says, "my child bride…"

I was confused by his statement but concerned because I knew that we had to get off this tram or the three of us would have to walk from the tram holding area if the doors closed on us. So, I ask again if they needed assistance, and he tells me they had just returned from the vacation of their lives. "We've never had a vacation like this," he says. "You see, my wife was given two weeks to live… three weeks ago. So, we have done everything in the last three weeks of her life that we always talked about doing, teased each other about, fantasized about but never had the money to do. Things we feared doing because of other people's opinions about what and where we were doing our thing." He says again, "My child bride just left me, and I'm going miss her so." It was then I realized what the smell was.

I am so glad I didn't opt out.

The Tram Ride... I opted in

You see, this couple of 70 years had set off three weeks ago for a two-week trip. They'd left home with a single brown paper bag of items between them, the clothes on their back, and the shoes on their feet. They were thinking that they would muster up at least one hiking trip, to take in the beauty of all God's wonders below them once they reached the pinnacle. Then they planned to sit along the beach enjoying the miraculous gift that God allowed them to witness: the sand, the sun, the moon, the water and most importantly "the people watching."

What started out as a modest hiking trip ended up being a 20-mile hiking adventure zip lining, bungee jumping, cliff diving and a near death experience with a black bear. They slept under the stars, snuggled next to a fire he had made; that brought back memories of when they used to go camping with their children, and then later, with their grandchildren. They made ever-sweet love to the sounds and cadences of the wild in the night.

Basking in the sun while lying on the beach seemed to give her an energy that she had not experienced in years. They snorkeled, went whale watching and witnessed baby sea turtles hatching. They even won the grand prize for a sand castle contest: One Night - All Expense paid stay at the best hotel on the beach.

They shared their life & love story with young couples and baby sat two-year-old twins, while the twins' parents battled another couple in a Karaoke contest. They enjoyed the chance to reminisce as they sang the oldies and goodies from days' past. They made ever-sweet love to the sound of the ocean's tides crashing while the moon light shone into their room. As the days and weeks past, she had miraculously felt better than she had in years but now, they were reminded of her illness as she began feeling fatigued; her medication had run out. It was time to return home.

They caught my eye as they boarded the tram. Had never seen either of them before but they seemed to fit perfectly together with their clothes tattered and shoes run over.

I am quickly intrigued by these two, their closeness, their oneness, her sitting almost in his lap. He welcomes her, accepts, and clearly responds to her in a way that is... that is more... than attentive. It is like a love affair. They steal kisses and look into each other's eyes as if no one else is around.

As her breathing becomes shallow and he supports her weight, he holds her close. She begins to convulse. Her hand lands on his lap and he reaches up to feel for her heartbeat. They keep their faces close, touching one another sharing the last minutes…, sharing the last seconds of their lives together. She slowly slips away. Life leaves her body. "**That smell…?**" The smell of death surrounds them.

a peace...
to heal and to forgive

Destiny

My battle scars?

ummh… I call them *beauty marks*
    they are where they are
    because of where I've been   and
    I gotta tell you that I've been around
    a few times and back again

My journey unique?
well… life's been no crystal stair
    I'm just grateful for the opportunity
    to have been there   and now
    just more aware

My future holds…?

My future holds Positivity!

Relatively,

what I seek from it *(my future that is)*…
is what it seeks from me

because my beauty marks…

    my   beauty   marks

    … they mark my destiny!

A New Me

There was something
　　　i was dying to tell you

but sat back in my seat
　　　and tried to get comfortable instead
　　　...heading to more cold weather
　　　but weather like California stuck in
　　　my head

i let the sun come in through the window...

shine on my face, trickle down my neck
　　　and rest on my collarbone

　　　　　...caught a chill
　　　　　wondering... reminiscing & recognizing

　　　　　that i... had grown

traveling with only the shoes i have on,
a pair of pants, an extra blouse...
but forgot my sleepwear

guess i'll use the scarf i always keep near..

to keep my neck warm or cover my head...

to cover up when i get out of the shower, and
i'll just wear it to bed

...caught a chill
wondering... reminiscing & recognizing

that i... had grown

thankful for my trip to Ohio and this new me...

i have found

Embracing Self

I sit   and love

I sit   and look and stare

I sit   and hate

I sit   and accept and respect

I sit   and laugh and long

I sit and cry   yes... I cry

I sit and love   I sit   and   love

but ultimately...I sit and embrace

I embrace myself   I   EMBRACE
ME

I embrace myself for who I was
I embrace myself for who I am
I embrace myself for who   I   AM   NOT
I embrace myself for who   I   WILL
BECOME

I love me...   I am beautiful   and
I am Fearfully and Wonderfully Made

I AM EMBRACING   SELF

Just a shell?

a shell of a dream
a shell of a family
a shell of a life
the reality of fear

a shell of hope
a shell of love
a shell of success
the remnants of memories

a shell of ideas
a shell of goals
a shell of plans
the painful reality

...a shell   of a Life

(photo taken by K. Martindavis)

S.O.S.

stop and look

if you dare

stop a minute

and simply stare

...at our devastation

our frustration

our constant battle

and attempts for preservation

can't they see   our desperation

and understand our need for conversation?

it's not all about compensation

but...

are we the wrong classification?

we've been reduced to and are beyond
...humiliation

some transitioned... *(RIPP)*

...some moved

and landed in a new destination

the rest of us

...feel we're destined for damnation

(S.O.S. we are dying down here)

(photo taken by K. Martindavis)

77

Uprooted In/Out of New Orleans

uprooted

        and... disconnected

maybe

just maybe

I'll grow new roots...?

(photo taken by K. Martindavis)

Cancer vs. a Different *Cancer*

Some people are fighting to live
while others…

are dying without a fight

Artik XI

The truth…

is
not
behind
what
you
say…

it's behind what you do

Artik XII

Don't block your blessing
trying
to teach someone else a lesson

"vengeance is mine," says the Lord

It's in There

words

are not   always   necessary
it's all in the eyes   yes?

connection/reflection - bonded
love… deep rooted

he sees   and remembers you all

you visit him in his dreams
(inthenightasthemoonglows&inthedayasthesunshines)

he calls   and you answer
you call   and he answers

he feels the love
in your unwavering presence
the warmth…   in your touch

and his heart
his heart thanks you for
relentless dedication and commitment

words

are not   always   necessary
it's all in the eyes   yes?

Mine

this life   of   mine

is...

this
life
of   mind

mine...   beingtheoperative   word
and i...   amgoodwithit

and
so
shall
you

be

IT: A Battered Woman's Battle Cry

IT may   or may not be your story
...and IT might   or might not be mine

but

IT just may be   **her**   **painandworry**

and we are not going to treat IT like we are
blind

Lord knows...   that there are some
testimonies
and HE knows...   that there are still some to
be recognized

No need to scream or shout because HE hears
your BATTLE CRY
Scream and shout if you must but HE hears
your BATTLE CRY

IT may have been just for days or weeks
and
IT might have lasted for years or even decades

you may be
or might   have been weighed down with
fearshameguiltangeror sadness
and felt you   were   just   about...   *(to die)*

No need to scream or shout because HE hears
your BATTLE CRY
Scream and shout if you must but HE hears
your BATTLE CRY

GOD

JEHOVAH JIREH *(the Lord Will Provide)*
ELOHIM *(Creator, Mighty/Strong)*
EL OLAM *(Everlasting God)*
EL-SHADDAI *(God Almighty)*
YAHWEH-RAPHA *(the Lord Who Heals)*
JEHOVAH SHALOM *(the Lord is Peace)*

HE… hears your battle cry!

HE… hears my battle cry!

HE… hears her battle cry!

HE… loves you most!

HE… loves you best!

and only HE can take care of IT!

Gaze

you say

i see r i g h t t h r o u g h y o u

right down to your soul

don't worry,   i'll keep your secrets...

noonewilleverknow

my gaze, they say is piercing

grandaddy gave it to me   years ago

there's power in the look & stare

makes some, tell all they know

don't worry about what i'm gonna say

noonewilleverknow

i'll keep your secrets every day

right down in my soul

Artik XIII

Do you know
that you make

a

difference?

sometimes, simply being present... is enough

Artik XIV

you may not know or realize it…

but
it
all
matters

(it really does)

Deliverance

My Lord…
i thank you for consideration

… my forgiven transgressions   and

transformation

this new relation

allows me

proclamation of
my regeneration
and
my sanctification

and thus….

SALVATION!

Lil' One

Little fingers, little toes
he'll be missed but only God knows

Only God knows how to heal the pain
and only God knows how to stop the rain

Only God knows the reason
and the Word says for all things,
there is a season

We just have to understand
that when we have our season,
only God knows the reason

The reason we exist
why some lives end early
while others persist

Why life's highways and byways
have the bends and turns

Why there are so many things in life
that cause us concern

The pieces of the puzzle seemingly
don't always fit
but God knows… He loves us
and wants us to hold on and not quit

He's right there
where He's always been
...we just have to open our hearts
and lives - and invite Him in

Then...
we can better understand
that when we have our season,
we can trust that God knows the reason

God knows how to heal the pain
and only
God knows how to stop the rain

Thank You

Sometimes we have to cleanse our minds
like we cleanse our bodies

thanks
for
the
laxative

Peace of Mind

My place in time
my peace of mind

both have me wonderingpondering

will I
       ever find mine

I feel the
achespainslovehatebloodstrains
lovedeceptioncommitmentperception.

I...

i
cannot run and leave behind...

iwannalivecryscreamlove&sometimes die,

are you

        blind?

The Cost

"Only"   adds up

and

eventually

will cost

you

more

than

you

bargained

for

Start Over

Sometimes...

we need to have a

b
 r e
          ak

      do
        w n

in order to have a

b r e a k   t h r o u g   h

then we can recognize
our...

New Beginning

Rain

i   love rain

it's **cleansing…**

it often allows   but

sometimes forces us

to purge our minds and spirits…

it holds us captive against our will…

demanding

that we   simply

stand

s   t   i l l …

        and face   ourselves

Artik XV

i...

forgive me

(that's so necessary!)

97

Artik XVI

i just might be going through the motions
but at least i am in motion

*we need to give others credit for the progress
that they make... going through the motions is
still movement*

Testimony

The **tests**
that cause us to **moan** the most...

will yield our greatest

TEST - I - MON - Y

That Cross

That cross you wear
…is the burden you have to bear

GOD will allow us to go through
so that we can recognize and be aware

…of HIS GRACE AND HIS MERCY

and that HE will never leave us
but…

will always be near

Your Reality

it's important

to understand
who you really are   and

to accept if you can, or need to be

...a better you

Look Up

sometimes…

GOD has to s l o w u s d o w n
(and put us on our backs)

so that we will look up
instead of being focused on

what's   in front of us

The Death of a Relationship

I am not sure how or why   and

I am not exactly sure

that it happened the way it *appeared*

but

I am positive that

i am sorry

it *appeared*

the way

you

saw

IT

Artik XVII

you
will find it

and

you
will recognize it

because

HE... is going to show it to you

Artik XVIII

when we
expect people
to respect us for
who and what we
are, we have to expect
to be willing to also
respect them for
who and what
they are

*this seems like a no brainer… but it's not
practiced*

The Beauty of The Color Red

I saw her come into the restaurant. She looked flushed; she looked sort of …uneasy. I was thinking that she looked like I normally feel this time of the day, rushed & hungry. Getting a quick bite to eat was seemingly where she was directing all her energy. She sat her large, over-stuffed bag in the seat next to her.

The restaurant was crowded and there was an unusual number of kids & patrons in general for this time of the day. A few minutes later, two employees led a group of children to a designated section where there was a birthday party about to begin. At that moment, a pretty, little chocolate girl with short hair emerged from the crowd. She was passing out party favors to her guests and seemed to know which color bag to give to each of them. Each child smiled widely as they received their gifts.

Obviously, the parents obliged and dressed their child in at least one garment which was the color red. Just then, I overheard two of the little boys talking as they walked back from the bathroom, "Yeah, my daddy said that I had swag when I put on this red sweater that my mom bought for me. I told him that I liked it and wanted to wear it to the party because it's her favorite color. You know that she's my girlfriend?" He said as the other boy nodded his head acknowledging that he was aware that the birthday girl was spoken for.

As I began to laugh to myself about what I had just heard, I noticed the young lady in the corner and for the first time, the flower in her hair. She reminded me of myself, quite a few years ago. I am assuming by her reaction she also heard the exchange between the two little boys, but she was not laughing. As she sat and watched the kids attentively, there was something in her eyes... something in the way she sat and pretended to eat the super-sized meal and dessert she had ordered. Something in the coincidence that she too wore red, made her stand out.

As the two employees led the birthday girl and party guests to the playground area, the young lady in the corner began to move quickly. She reached into her bag and pulled out what seemed to be five wrapped presents. She darted toward the gift table and the birthday girl's mother was startled by the young lady's sudden movement. The mother's facial expression changed quickly and her body language indicated that she knew the young lady; they embraced one another. I clearly was not the only one to notice their exchange as they walked away from the other parents, who were apparently intrigued. They walked closer to where I sat.

"I'm so glad you could make it," the mother said. "I wouldn't have missed it" said the young lady from the corner. The mother asked, "Did I mention the color scheme was red? And the flower? Why did you put a red rose bud in your hair?" The young lady's voice cracked, "I don't know why I put the flower in my hair, but I love roses and red is simply my favorite color, always has been." Just then, the kids returning from the play area seemed to force the young lady to retreat to her corner table.

As they sang Happy Birthday to the little girl, I noticed the young lady in the corner sang the hardest. I am not sure why, but I was quite touched by this. Just then, everyone told the birthday girl to make a wish… she closed her eyes and made her wish. As she opened her eyes… *(maybe I was the only one who noticed)* the birthday girl gently reached up with her right hand and touched herself in the spot where the heart lies. She then touched the red rose bud in her hair and instinctively… her eyes drifted to the corner where the young lady sat.

My Sister

When I see you...   I see me

I see **we**
as the ones that are looking out and
looking in...   looking beyond the color of
skin

looking into the depths
of the pains   and the joys
not always knowing
that sometimes

   ... the pains are the joys

and the joys...   are!

they are what we make them

and sometimes
we have to simply share the joys of others
because we don't always see our own... joys

as big or small as they are
                        my sister – they are

and I am   tickled

                              pink

Sinful

It almost   felt like a sin *(a sin I tell you)*
not to bring the new year in

to the smell of black eyed-peas,
some variation of cabbage or greens
…and some   swine.

I…   yes   I,
broke tradition and made   lasagna.

Sister said, "Girl, you know Grams is turning
over in her grave and what… what did Mommy
say?"

My weak reply,

"Well,   I didn't lie… plus   I am grown!
I…   I told her that I was having some… but
didn't say that I was cooking it."

"ANYWAY… Mommy is getting old, and she
probably didn't cook all that stuff this year
herself."

Sister said "Oh yeah…, she cooked it and so
did I."

Well...,

I... wasn't going to be hog-tied into fixing all the things that Mommy and Grams were committed to cook over the years, and seemed blasphemous not to.

Now...,

I did get an invite and decided to go to a friend's house to help them eat the traditional meal their mother had fixed.

As I was greeted at the door, I could smell and feel the love...

I could hear the chatter and the laughter... the cling, clanging of the dishes... the pots and pans.

This...

this - feels like home
feels   like   Grandma's house

smells

like... Grandma's.

As I thanked God for the opportunity to share this meal...

a tear   came out   of   somewhere.

With a forkful of morsels in my mouth...
the realization... that this meal

marked a new year. *(one not promised – RIPP)*

I secretly began counting my blessings with each

in

                        di

        vid   u

                              al

black eyed pea I ate. That's what you're supposed to do.

I secretly began searching through my cabbage...

for the coins that should be hiding, waiting to spring forth on some expecting person's fork...

to mark a prosperous year.

I secretly prayed…
I prayed,
that each bite of chitterling I ate would propel
me into a more progressive state of mind.

That meal,
that meal I ate…

was food for my soul.

And the ambiance…
the ambiance I enjoyed…

was good for my soul.

But I have to say…

I just gotta say it…

"someone needs to repent…

for forgetting the Franks RedHot Hotsauce

just plain…

sinful!"

Dear Lovie

i died a tragic death today and i can see my body still has not been found by anyone. i now wish that i had gone on that football trip with my boys - all of them. It seems like days have passed since the accident but it only happened earlier today.

i just had to go to the beach by myself... one last time!

You know Lovie, as i was slipping away and only had a little time to pray *(because i fought and panicked so hard)*, i asked God to keep and protect my family. i asked Him to send them someone who would love them all just as i had, although... she could never replace me.

He said "Done."

Then i asked God to expand the territory of all those whom i had ever come in contact with... in every aspect, beginning with the expansion of their relationship with Him.

He said "Done."

Lovie, i thanked God with seemingly my last breath for all the gracious things he had done for me. He'd given me a loving family and close friends. He'd blessed me with a life that wasn't full of tragedy, pain or sorrow, but one of continual blessings that were quite evident, but not always acknowledged.

He said "are you Done?"

For some reason Lovie, i looked at my watch and realized that it was the "Eleventh Hour" and i asked God to have mercy upon me. i began repenting of my sins, sins Lovie that i knew i had committed but tried throughout my life to forget, or pretend that i had not committed. i'm talking lies i told as a child and lies i told as an adult.

Shoot... you were there on 1st Sunday when i told that lie that so many of us tell every Sunday - that i knew without a shadow of a doubt, knowing that it wasn't true. i asked for forgiveness for the things i had stolen including the pens they will find at the bottom of my purse that i have taken from random places or random people.

And although i couldn't distinguish them from the salt water engulfing me, warm tears ran down my face as i asked God to forgive me for the murders i had committed. You do realize Lovie that killing someone doesn't <u>always</u> mean taking their life?

i didn't realize that i had so many issues that needed to be addressed... and no that wasn't a lie!

He said "I know."

So i repented for my covetousness, disobedience, sexual immoralities and the list went on but after all of this...

He said **"Done!"**

Lovie, i was so grateful for that "Eleventh Hour" but wouldn't recommend it; it's too risky!

Well, they have found my body. Just like on TV, no matter how long you've been under, they always try to resuscitate you. Although, they have no idea that i had been under (submerged in life), for quite a long time and there wasn't anything that anyone except **The One** could do for me.

They are about to contact my next of kin and it's about to get real emotional, so i will prepare to close for now but, i promise to keep in contact. Oh, one last thing...

You've probably been wondering why i've been calling you Lovie; well, that's my new name for you. i've come to realize that you sure do like to love others. Well, maybe i said that wrong, maybe i should have said that you sure do like to be loved by others. But know and understand Lovie, that loving others without loving God...

by itself,

... is never enough!

Artik XIX

Only God…

loves
me

more

The End

Some *peaces* as written... may seem
incomplete.

But it might be so that **you** can finish it.
What is your ending to the story or poem...?

Poetry is not... *just words,*
not just the concept of putting pen to paper.

Poetry can be a state of mind...
             a state of emotion...
             a state of physical or mental
             being or... *the perception of.*

And poetry can be an awareness of
             a state of spiritual need.

Thank you for sharing

             my state... of *peace*

and welcome

             ...to your state of completion.

71193466R00083

Made in the USA
Columbia, SC
25 May 2017